Enrico Massetti

Sicily

Enrico Massetti

Copyright Enrico Massetti 2015

Published by Enrico Massetti

ISBN: 978-1-329-29871-2

Sicily

An incredible fusion of races, civilizations and systems of government; an unexpected interweaving of customs and habits; and an ever-changing and astonishing variety of landscapes with volcanoes and forests, seas and mountains are the attractions which await the tourist on his long journey from Naples to the wonders of Sicily.

The itinerary:

The itinerary

From REGGIO CALABRIA where we can arrive by air or driving we take the ferry across the straits, and land at MESSINA.

Messina

Duomo

Messina: a few hours will suffice to visit this city which was almost completely destroyed and rebuilt twice in this century: after the earthquake in 1908 and the bombardments in 1943, Of the original Norman structure of the Cathedral (1168) only the lower part of the facade and the magnificent Gothic portals have remained (inside, remains of ancient mosaics in the apse).

Nearby is the church of SS. Annunziata dei Catalani, an elegant combination of Romanesque and Arab-Norman architecture, with a remarkable Apse. We should also visit the important National Museum in the former church of San Gregorio. Noteworthy are: a Polyptych by Antonello do Messina, works by his pupils, two fine paintings by Caravaggio, works by Mattia Preti, ancient, medieval, and Renaissance sculptures, among the latter some by Lantana.

Santa Maria Alemanna

The church dates back to the second half of the 13th century and was founded, together with an adjacent hospital, by the teutonic Knights, thus explaining the name "Alemanna", by which it is still known.

The knights set up their priory here and used the hospital to receive and tend veterans from the Holy Land. Only a small trace of the ancient hospital remains, in the form of a lancer arch and a fragment of wall near the apses of the church. The church itself, abandoned by the knights at the end of the 14th century, was struck by lightning at the beginning of the 17th century, and was further damaged in the earthquake of 1783, which caused the facade to collapse.

Today it is under restoration, after having been dismantled stone by stone to allow consolidation. The regional museum contains a fine portal from this church which is the purest example of Gothic architecture in Sicily, since it was built using entirely G e r m a n   m e t h o d s .
The knights hospital, which later passed to the Confraternita dei Rossi, admitted a famous patient after the battle of Lepanto in 1571, in the person of the great Miguel Saavedra Cervantes.

Santissima Annunziata dei Catalani

The church of the "Annunziata dei Catalani" stands on one of the most historically important sites of the Straits. Nearby, there was once the Byzantine shipyard, guarded by the fortress of Castellamare. The church was built between 1150 and 1200 on the remains of a pagan temple dedicated to Neptune. It is an interesting example of how various architectural styles were added to a late Byzantine construction typical of those built by the Basilian Order of monks. The blind loggias and the play of color created by the exterior stonework, along with the two-tone arches of the interior and the elongated layout of the church, are all indications of Islamic and Byzantine influence, and also reflect contemporary architecture on mainland Italy.

The original length of the naves was almost double their present length: they were shortened and the facade was redone following a flood in the Middle Ages, which caused the front section of the church to collapse.

The church has been known by the name "Catalani" ever since the 16th century, when the senate of Messina gave it to the powerful guild of the Catalan merchants. The guild made it their headquarters and placed the coats of arms of Catalonia on the main entrance. The great difference in height between the ground level of the church and that of the surrounding streets and buildings is due to the piles of rubble caused by the earthquake of 1908, which were later leveled for reconstruction.

The Cathedral

Duomo

The church was originally built in Norman times, but only in 1197, in a ceremony presided over by Henry VI of Swabia (the father of Frederick II, who lived and was buried in Messina), was it dedicated to the Virgin Mary.

Nothing of the Norman construction remains today except the general layout and the overall exterior appearance which, after the 1908 earthquake, the architect Valenti reconstructed on the basis of ancient documents.

Since at least the 14th century the Cathedral has undergone various structural changes.

Guidotto de Tabiatis, the bishop whose tomb, sculpted by Goro di Gregorio in 1333, can be admired in the transept- ordered the construction of an additional section, along the south front of the cathedral, decorated with black and white stone bands and beautiful mullioned windows.

The 14th century also saw the addition of the baptismal font by Florentine Gaddo Gaddi and the mosaics in the vaults of the apses. These depict, from south to north: St Giovanni between St Nicola and St. Basilio; Christ Pantocrator; and the Virgin and Child between, Archangels, St Lucia and St Agata. The three portals of the Cathedral facade, with their elaborate decorations in polychrome bands and sculpted features, date from the same period. The central portal is by Baboccio da Piperno and shows figures of kings and saints, cherubs intently observing a mystic harvest, heraldic devices and symbols of the Evangelists. The triangular gable with God the Father at the top and a tondo depicting Christ crowning the Virgin were added in 1468 by Pietro di Bonate. The statue of Madonna and Child, in the lunette of the portal, is from 1534, and is the work of Giovambattista Mazzeo.

The 16th century saw radical intervention also inside the building: Montorsoli designed a marble inlay floor and the arrangement, along the walls of the side naves, representing the Apostolate.

The sculptor from Carrara, Andrea Calamech, sculpted the marble pulpit, and Jacopo Lo Duca built the chapel of the Sacrament in the north apse. The canopy in wood and copper and the high altar in mixed marble act as a kind of theatrical device to focus attention on the painting of the Madonna della Lettera (patron saint of Messina), and date bach to the 17th century. The altar, designed by Simone Gulli – who was also responsible for a unique series of buildings along the port known as the "Maritime Theatre", was begun in 1628 and finished at the end of the 18th century. A large number of artists collaborated on its construction, including the great goldsmiths of the Juvarra family, who also made the other altar, in silver and gold, built into the modern one at the center of the transept, depicting the Virgin handing over her letter to the ambassadors of Messina.

In 1930, the Cathedral became home to what is the largest organ in Italy and the third largest in Europe: 5 keyboards, 170 stops, 16000 pipes arranged in both sides of the transept, behind the altar, above the main portal and above the triumphal arch.

The bell-tower of the Cathedral

Duomo Bell Tower

At the beginning of the 16th century, Martino Montanini planned what was to be, at 90 meters, the highest bell-tower in Sicily.

Struck by lightning in 1588, it was rebuilt by Andrea Calamech in around 1575. The base of the belltower originally housed the city archives, which were taken by the Spanish in 1678 and transported to Seville, where they remain to this day.

The old bell-tower, damaged in the earthquake of 1783, was demolished soon afterwards. The present tower, designed by Valenti, imitates the forms of its predecessor.

It was built after 1908, and in 1933 became home to the largest animated clock in the world, work of the Ungerer brothers from Strasbourg.

Fountain of Nettuno

Fountain of Nettuno

The splendid monumental fountain representing Nettuno were built in 1557 by Fra' Giovanni Angelo da Montorsoli, on commission of the Senate of Messina and in close collaboration with the great humanist and local mathematician Francesco Maurolico.

The fountain of Nettuno is a assimilation of the powerful style of Michelangelo in sculpture. The figure of the god rises calm and invincible, holding his terrible trident with its power to shake the earth; the monstrous Scilla and Cariddi chained at is feet, hurl animal screams.

The fountain, which in the 16th century was situated only a few feet from the sea, with Nettuno turned towards the city, was designed to be seen with the blue backdrop of the harbor, as if the figures had just risen from the water, and as if the god was laying claim to the city.

Gallery and Theatre Vittorio Emanuele

Galleria Vittorio Emanuele

The Galleria inaugurated in 1939, the building represents the major work of the local civil engineer and architect Camillo Puglisi Allegra, an important figure in the eclectic school of architecture.

This building is one of only two examples of its kind in the south of Italy, the other being the gallery in Naples. Puglisi Allegra, who personally designed all the decorations (sculpted by the artists Bonfiglio and Lovetti), drew inspiration from 18th century Sicilian Art.

The extremely elegant effect was completed by the decorations in wrought iron, multicolored windows and carefully designed lighting, based on lamps hidden behind cornices to give an effect of sheet light.

The Theatre up until 1861 called the Sant'Elisabetta theatre, this building is the only example in the historic center, and one of the few in the city as a whole, of neoclassical architecture.

It was constructed in 1852 according to the plans of the Neapolitan Pietro Valente, assisted by the local architect, Carlo Falconieri.

The earthquake of 1908 left the building seriously unsafe, and the hall and stage (mostly wooden constructions) were subsequently lost. Between 1911 the rear section of the theatre was extended, to create a small auditorium still in use today, named after the local musician, Antonio Laudamo. The new theatre, which retains the perimeter walls of the front section with their neoclassical stuccoes and decorations, was not reopened to the public until 1985.

Inside, the ceiling is decorated with the "Legend of Colapesce" by Renato Guttuso.

Santa Maria della Valle, the "Badiazza"

The "Badiazza"

The ruins of the antique church and convent of Santa Maria della Valle, commonly said "Badiazza", forms one the most antique and interesting monuments of the Medieval Messina. It is placed on the bottom of the San Rizzo, stream and is reached by the trunk-road of the Peloritani mountains passing a difficult road trough the village Scala, and going upstream the pebbly river- bed. It belonged to a Benedictine monastery founded most likely in the 12th century. Some historians believe that it was built in the 12th century or at the beginning of the following century, near or over previous Roman constructions of which traces were found. After the devastation of the fire in 1282, it was most likely restored in the 14th century a small furnace was built nearby, which used the calcareous stone blocks of the building damaged it even more.

It has a basilicas plant with three naves with a wide antuary and a hight transept with three apses; higher than the rest of the church and in the middle of it a spherical cusp, now fallen, was raised held by four huge pillars.

This planimetry recalls – for similarity – that of other Messenese's Churches, particularly the one of SS. Annunziata of the Catalani with whom it would have the cusps in common. But this one was elevated on cylindrical pendentives, while the one of the Santa Maria della Valle is elevated on pillars with degraded small arches of which clear traces have remained.

On the four angles of the sanctuary, at the height of the cusp impost, there were square rooms, which were most likely used as women's gallery. Quadrilobate pillars hold the ribbed vaults of the nave; the capitals are of various composition. On the outside, the monument presents itself as a single blocked mass, geometrically composed; the Gothic windows in regular order, and the merlon completion give the church a reinforced civil construction appearance.

Aeolian Islands

Before leaving Messina we advise paying a visit to the nearby Aeolian Islands, with their wild rocky coasts falling sheer into the sea; there are seven of them – Lipari, Vulcano, Salina, Panarea, Stromboli, Filicudi and Alicudi; they are ideal for a holiday that is different and fascinating.

Lipari

The Aeolian islands (Isole Eolie) are a group of attractive islands in the Tyrrhenian Sea about 25-50km north of Sicily in Italy. Formerly off the beaten track, this diverse group of volcanic islands is becoming more popular and can be very busy during July and August.

The Islands

- Lipari – the main island and the main town (called Lipari as well) is the transport hub, with plenty of hotels and makes a good base.

- Vulcano – right next to Lipari, this island is dominated by the *Gran Cratere* volcano cone giving off clouds of sulfurous gas. This peak gives great views. The island is popular for its beaches and *mud baths*.

- Salina is lush and hilly – great for a relaxing walk. Some of the film *Il Postino* was shot here.

- Panarea – a smaller, upmarket island with great views across to *Stromboli*.

- Stromboli – the most remote of the islands, it is little more than a volcano rising out of the sea. Popular for trips out at night to see magma spurting out of the cone.

- Filcudi and Alicudi lie to the West and are much less visited, particularly Alicudi, which is still primarily agrarian.

Communication

Although local dialects of Sicilian are spoken among the locals, the traveler will find that standard Italian is also spoken by most people he will encounter. Those involved in the tourist trade may also speak some English, German, or French. Cellular telephone coverage is dependable in the settled areas, but access to the internet is rare. There are a few internet cafes in Lipari Town.

Where to eat in Lipari:

Restaurants in Lipari:

- Naghet Cafe Via Mazzini, Acquacalda, +39 335 100 3510 A nice quiet cafe with very friendly service. A good spot to relax and have a drink. A very cozy spot with a wonderful view, adorable chill out music to release yourself. Regarding the staff, a friendly treatment and always helpful all the time.
- Gilberto e Vera Via Garibaldi 22, +39 090 981 2756 This is a small deli/wine bar which offers a fantastic range of panini for lunch. Seat outside and watch the Lipari world go by as you have yours. If you only lunch once in Lipari then lunch here!
- Marisa Via Stradale Pianoconte, +39 090 982 2243 Lovely family owned restaurant where you eat excellent home cooked food. You can find fresh, good quality fish of the day or one of the restaurants Italian specialities like rabbit cooked in sweet and sour sauce. The choice in the menu is very limited, which I find good, they do few things, but really well! There is also a big antipasti buffet with various choices of home cooked dishes. In the kitchen, there is Marisa cooking, a real " Italian mama" and the pastries are all made by her husband who has a real passion for creating with sweets. Choices of wine is tasteful.
- E' Pulera Via Isabella Conti Vainicher +39 090 981 1158 This restaurant is more up market than the ones down by the port and the prices are higher. Service is fantastic, with the owner making great suggestions for you. Courgette flowers stuffed with Ricotta are to die for and Cassata for dessert is outstanding. There is a large selection of fish and pasta for mains using local produce. Lovely food.
- Chimera Via Falcone e Borsellino, +39 090 981 1934 Restaurant is located in the MEA hotel and offers a glorious setting. The atmosphere is fascinating, with a beautiful view on the harbor. Food is of a superior level and dishes presentation is very accurate. Quantity can be considered a bit poor and price high as compared to restaurants of same level.
- Trattoria del Vicolo Vicolo Vico Ulisse 16/17, +39 090 981 1066 Situated down a small lane off the Main Street, this

restaurant has great ambience, really good service and the food is fantastic. No English menu, however there is one waiter that speaks a little English which really helps when ordering. The rolled eggplant is amazing along with the swordfish. Good wine list. Gets very busy, would recommend you book on Friday or Saturday nights.

- La Conchiglia Via T. M. Amendola, +39 090 981 3119 Friendly service and a good selection presented of local freshly caught fish. Service is good and food nicely prepared and presented. Unfortunately around 9 pm they tie a large ferry boat up on quay next to Restaurant blocking what is a ver nice view across the harbor.
- Ristorante Filippino Piazza Mazzini, +39 090 981 1002 The family running this business is so passionate about what they do. As a company that has been around for 105 years now you can trust that they are true professionals. The dish you would like may not be there the day you visit because working with the fresh fish of the night they never know what fish will be cached, in fact, the menu is done daily as a result of the night's catch.
- Papisca Via Marina Garibaldi, 67, +39 090 981 2362 Local cafe that's open late -- seems to be the town watering hole. Desserts & bar. Beautiful food for lunches, all homemade! All Sicilian specialities are presented on the day, excellent gelatos - the best on the island, big cappuccinos, quick and kind staff.
- Villa Liberty Isa Conti Ellen, +39 090 981 4270 The location of the restaurant is a nice garden, very close to Lipari's center, but out from the crowd. The food is very good and tasty. Prices vs quality is good. The owner and the staff are very gentle and nice.

Vulcano

Vulcano

Vulcano is one of the Aeolian Islands. Famous for its mud bath, the island literally smells like rotten eggs (sulphur).

Vulcano is a small volcanic island in the Tyrrhenian Sea, about 25 km north of Sicily and the southernmost of the Aeolian Islands.

It is 21 square kilometers in area, rises to 499 meters, and contains several volcanic centers, including one of four active non-submarine volcanoes in Italy and the formerly separate islet of **Vulcanello**.

Vulcano History

The Greek wind god Aeolus was said to have lived on this island, then called *Hiera'*. The name for the entire Aeolian Island chain descended from the mythical residence of Aeolus.

The Roman name for the island Vulcano has contributed the word for *volcano* in most modern European languages. The Romans used the island mainly for raw materials, harvesting wood and mining alum and sulfur. This was the principal activity on the island until the end of the 19th Century.

When the Bourbon rule collapsed in 1860 (see Francis II of the Two Sicilies) a British man named James Stevenson bought the northern part of the island, built a villa, reopened the local mines and planted vineyards for grapes that would later be used to make Malvasia wine. Stevenson lived on Vulcano until the last major eruption on the island, in 1888. The eruption lasted the better part of two years, by which time Stevenson had sold all of his property to the local populace, and never returned to the island. The villa is still intact. It is at an hydrofoil ride from Lipari and has several hotels and cafes, the important attractions being the beaches, hot springs and sulfur mud baths.

Vulcano Geology

The volcanic activity in the region is largely the result of the northward-moving African Plate meeting the Eurasian Plate. There are three volcanic centers on the island:

- At the southern end of the island are old stratovolcano cones, Monte Aria (500 m), Monte Saraceno (481 m) and Monte Luccia (188 m), which have partially collapsed into the Il Piano Caldera.

- The most recently active center is the Gran Cratere at the top of the Fossa cone, the cone having grown in the Lentia Caldera in the middle of the island, and has had at least 7 major eruptions in the last 6000 years.

- At the north of the island is Vulcanello, 123 meters high, and is connected to the rest of it by an isthmus which is flooded in bad weather. It emerged from the sea during an eruption in 183 BC as a separate islet. Occasional eruptions from its three cones with both pyroclastic flow deposits and lavas occurred from then until 1550, the last eruption creating a narrow isthmus connecting it to Vulcano. Vulcano has been quiet since the eruption of the Fossa cone on August 3, 1888 to 1890, which deposited about 5 meters of pyroclastic material on the summit. The style of eruption seen on the Fossa cone is called a Vulcanian eruption, being the explosive emission of pyroclastic fragments of viscous magmas caused by the high viscosity preventing gases from escaping easily.

Vulcano Mythology

Vulcano

The Romans believed that Vulcano was the chimney to the god Vulcanus's workshop. The island had grown due to his periodic clearing of cinders and ashes from his forge. The earthquakes that either preceded or accompanied the explosions of ash etc., were considered to be due to Vulcanus making weapons for Mars and his armies to wage war.

Expulsion of lava is a rare feature of Vulcan eruptions and always occur at the end of the eruption.

Since Roman times similar features on Earth have been known as volcans – volcanes and volcanoes. It is also used in connection with similar features on the Moon, Mars, Venus and Mercury and other stellar bodies. Some purists argue that the name should be vulcans, vulcanes and vulcanoes.

The Romans gave the word to the world and with it came ashes, cinders, lava – "flows."

Vulcano Boat round-trip

The tour of the Vulcano island starts from Porto di Levante, very well known for its fumaroles and its thermal springs. Following the tour towards north-west, you arrive in the small peninsula of Vulcanello. After the channel that divides Vulcano from Lipari direction south, you will see the amazing Grotto of the Horse, with its spectacular light effects. Then you arrive back to Porto di Levante.

Aeolian Islands: Getting There

There are frequent car ferries and much quicker hydrofoils from Milazzo and Messina on Sicily, and from Reggio di Calabria on the mainland, to and between the islands. Most call first at Lipari, and then proceed to the other islands. Ferries are frequent in Summer, with fewer during Spring, Autumn and Winter and on *Sundays*. For timetables see SIREMAR, at http://www.siremar.it/, Ustica Lines at http://www.usticalines.it/, and NGI at http://www.ngi-spa.it/. It is important to check the timetables in advance, and to allow plenty of time for connections, as boats can be early or late.

A few car ferries a week also continue on to Naples (see SNAV at http://www.snav.it/) and during the summer hydrofoils run to and from Naples, Cefalu, Palermo and Messina.

Lipari

The Aeolian Islands are quite remote, which is part of their appeal. No air travel is available to the archipelago, except for the very expensive helicopter service which runs during high season from the Catania airport. For more information see Air Panarea. Most international travelers, then, will arrive at the airport of either Palermo or Catania airport in Sicily, or Reggio di Calabria, across the straits of Messina on the mainland.

Although the Reggio airport is relatively near the port, boats from Reggio are infrequent. Likewise, only a few ferries per day run from Palermo during high season, and the airport is far from the city.

These ports are best used by the traveler who is already in Italy, as is Naples, a much longer boat trip that is convenient for travelers arriving by plane or train in Naples from points north.

For the traveler arriving directly from abroad, numerous budget airlines have routes from around Europe to Catania. From there, one can take the train, or an express bus, to Messina, connecting to a boat; or, at Messina, one can connect to a second train or bus to Milazzo, which has by far the most boat departures. Although it is convenient to change trains in Messina, the Milazzo train station is a few miles from the port. On the other hand, the bus from Catania arrives at the train station, while the bus for Milazzo departs from a separate bus station a few blocks away. Ask for help at the information booth outside the train station.

One express bus per day departs from Catania airport for Milazzo, but arrives there so late as to miss the boat for certain of the islands. One may wish to spend the first night in Lipari, with its charming town, and then depart for the outlying islands. As another alternative, the car rental agencies have special deals allowing the traveler the use of a car one-way from Catania to Milazzo – inquire in advance as these deals may not be available without reservations. The car rental agencies in Milazzo are a few blocks from the port.

Aeolian Islands: Getting Around

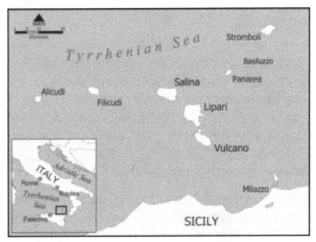

Aeolian Islands

The larger islands, Lipari, Vulcano and Salina have quite good bus services. Timetables are available at the tourist offices in each island's port. Those islands also have scooters for rent, and are the only of the islands with comprehensive systems of roads. Panarea and Stromboli are small enough to have no roads or automobiles to speak of; Panarea in particular is completely accessible by foot. Alicudi and Filicudi are so remote that they have little in the way of developed tourist industries or infrastructure.

On those islands, transport from the port, and scooter rental, should be arranged with one's innkeeper. Boat rental is also popular for touring the periphery of each island; although the small boats for rent are not adequate for travel between the islands, but are popular for the excursion from Panarea to the islets of Basiluzzo and Drauto.

After Messina one follows the impressive east coast of Sicily through citrus groves and little fishing villages among the rocks; on the other side of the Strait rises the coast of Calabria, dominated by the Aspromonte. After Capo S. Alessio and Forza d'Agro, perched on a high cliff, we reach (32 miles from Messina) Taormina-Giardini, from which we drive up to TAORMINA.

Taormina

Taormina

Taormina, one of the most beautiful places in Italy, situated on a terrace facing the sea and the snowy slopes of Mt. Etna. A Greek and later (4th century) a Roman colony, Taormina was destroyed and rebuilt by the Arabs and subsequently passed into the hands of the Normans in 1069. Its most important buildings date from the end of the Middle Ages, such as the delightful Tower of the Badia Vecchia, which dominates the town, the Cathedral, the Palazzo Santo Stefano and the crenellated Palazzo Corvaia which stands next to the 16th century church of S. Caterina.

From classical times there remain a few Greek wall and temple bases and, above all, the magnificent Greek Theatre, which was almost entirely rebuilt by the Romans and is the largest in Sicily after that in Syracuse.

Taormina and Mount Etna

Taormina has been a very popular tourist destination since the 19th century. It has popular beaches (accessible via an aerial tramway) on the Ionian sea, which is remarkably warm and has a high salt content. Taormina can be reached via highways (*autostrade*) from Messina from the north and Catania from the south.

Many exhibitions and events are organized during the summer in Taormina. The exceptional stage for pop and classical concerts, opera and important performances often recorded by television (for example, the ceremony of the Silver Ribbon Award, the Festivalbar, the Kore) is the Ancient Theatre. Since 1983, the most important performances are realized by Taormina Arte, the cultural institution which organizes one of the most famous music, theatre and dance festivals. Within the program of Taormina Arte there is the Taormina Film Fest, the well-known cinema festival, the heir of the Cinema Festival of Messina and Taormina, dating from 1960, which for about twenty years has hosted the David of Donatello Awards with the participation of the most famous Italian film stars. During the Taormina Film Fest the Silver Ribbons are now awarded, a prize created by Italian Film Journalists.

Since 2005, in October, Taormina Arte has organized the Giuseppe Sinopoli Festival, a festival dedicated completely to the great conductor, who died in 2001 and was for many years the artistic director of Taormina Arte.

Sicily's most spectacular resort, Taormina, hangs high above the sea with handy cable car access to the beach. Taormina was a favorite aristocratic escape in the 19th century. Today its main drag is made to order for good living. Enjoy the views, great people watching, and a freshly-filled cannoli.

Where to eat in Taormina:

Restaurants in Taormina:

- On the Road pub Via San Pancrazio 48, +39 0942 628 343 Not very noticable on the outside, however there is a 'hidden' roof terrace. The place is outside of crowded parts of Taormina, although not far away. Really good burgers,fine cocktails and kind staff. Pleasant atmosphere!

- DiBi Via Francavilla N. 197, Trappitello, +39 0942 58 149 The restaurant is quite spacious and furnished nicely, the staff is friendly and helpful. Dish are hamburgers, served in great variety with extensive customization options. Also good selection of beers and other dishes.

- Da Cristina Piazza del Duomo | Via strabone 2, +39 0942 21 171 A few hints: (1) Consider ordering off of the restaurant menu, even for take-away. They are delicious and take a little extra time but add to the variety of options. (2) Make sure you confirm what you order and pay for what you get. The Senora knows what she is doing, and enthusiastically helps the hapless foreigner through challenges, but her help staff are not as skilled at navigating the pressure and pace.

- L'Incontro Via Luigi Pirandello, 20, + 39 0942 628 084 You don't really go here for the view but for the excellent food and fantastically friendly and charming owner. Waitstaff also excels. A wide range of dishes cooked with care and love for

Sicilian food. Great value food and wine in a lovely atmospheric setting, terrific friendly service.

- Ristorante Cinque Archi Via S. Giovanni Bosco 39 (Piazza IX Aprile), +39 0942 628 722 This restaurant sits above a lively square near the end of the walk through the main shopping street above the Wunderbar cafe-bar. You have to negotiate some steep steps to get there but it´s worth it. The food is exquisite, the service very attentive and helpful and the views over the square with lively entertainment are fantastic.

- Villa Carlotta Restaurant Via Pirandello, 81 | Hotel Villa Carlotta, +39 0942 626 058 When you arrive in the restaurant, David (the head chef) and his staff will introduce themselves to you and tell you about the menu. You'll soon see that David is an extremely clever and dedicated chef, taking his inspiration from the best local produce and ancient Sicilian recipes to develop a very interesting, thoughtful and varied menu. The food is delicious and and beautifully presented. The real strength in David's menu is the compilation of dishes that let the ingredients speak for themselves without crowding each other or becoming unnecessarily complicated.

- Al Saraceno Via Madonna della Rocca,16/18, +39 0942 632 015 Fantastic restaurant at the top of Taormina by the church (Madonna Della Rocca). Great terrace with views over Castelmola, Etna and Giardini-Naxos. You can take a taxi to the top but there is a steep walkway up to the castle, however, this isn't lit up at night.

- Il Barcaiolo Via Castelluccio 43 | Spiaggia Mazzaro, +39 0942 625 633 A little tricky to find since it's almost at beach level down a long flight of steps not far from the cable car depot. This restaurant is worth finding. If the seafood was any fresher it would jump off the plate. Many of the dishes on the menu have a truly Sicilian spin on them. Keep in mind they are closed Tuesday's so ensure you're in town one of the other nights. Great value for money. Not to be missed a truly wonderful dining experience.

- <u>Lido La Caravella Club</u> C/Da Spisone | Directly on the beach, +39 0942 620 049 La Caravella is a gem on the beach, clean, friendly, well organized. The staff are very attentive, and Dominic leads with friendly charm and humor. Wonderful location, beautiful clear waters, you can spend a great day in one of the best secluded beaches in Sicily, it has a very good restaurant that provides good beach service and also for lunch to top it off, must visit!

- <u>Ristorante Da Andrea</u> Via Nazionale 159, +39 0942 628 760 The best restaurants have to be in the heart of Taormina...right? Yes, until you discover this hidden gem, tucked away on a side street. There is no spectacular view, nothing stand out about the atmosphere, in fact, when sitting inside you can think it is quite hot, however, the meal is nothing short of perfect.

Acireale

Acireale Santa Tecla

We shall remain in Taormina all of the next day, to enjoy its unrivaled beauty and relax after our journey through Calabria. In the morning, we continue down the coast skirting the foot of Mt. Etna. After 22 miles, we reach ACIREALE.

ACIREALE. Founded by the Greeks, then under Roman and Norman rule, Acireale was destroyed by two earthquakes and rebuilt in its present Baroque style which is to be noted particularly in the impressive and elaborately decorated church of San Sebastiano.

Acireale offers many leisure activities, which includes art, festivals and concerts, nature, open-air markets, theater, and thermal baths.

The church of San Biagio in Acireale contains some of the relics of the Venerable Gabriele Allegra, who had entered the Franciscan seminary in 1918.

Villa Belvedere and Parco delle Terme, two large public parks and "La Timpa", a beautiful natural reserve overlooking the Ionian Sea, offer great nature sights. Piazza Duomo, with its St. Peter's Basilica, is in the main square of the city.

There are many beautiful historic Baroque buildings in town, such as Palazzo Pennisi and Palazzo Modò, which date from the 17th century, and Palazzo Musmeci dating from the 18th century. The commercial city center is primarily located in the streets including and adjacent to *Corso Umberto* and *Corso Italia*, which are the city's principal thoroughfares.

Acireale is famous for its spectacular floats during the carnival season which attracts many visitors.

Another 10 miles and we come to CATANIA.

Where to eat in Acireale:

Restaurants in Acireale:
- Pizzeria Damm Di Messina Maria Antonia Domenica Via Salvatore Vigo 88, +39 095 605 260 If you are looking for a pizza with quality ingredients, seasoned well and at a good price you're at the right place! The menu is very extensive and includes pizzas and focacce to satisfy even the most demanding. The courtesy of the staff and the cleanliness of the room complete the picture!
- Vico Proiette Via Dafnica, 88, +39 095 763 7043 A very nice courtyard, where you eat a very good meal which is very well served. The inner courtyard is delightful. The dining room looks pretty smart as well, and in mid-October it is still very comfortable sitting outside.
- Verde Blu Via Santa Maria La Scala 52, +39 333 205 3533 It"s difficult to find but once you are there you will love it. One of the best fish restaurants around. No menu but they keep on serving so many delicious dishes from fish, seafood, pasta, they serve almost 20 dishes. It was fantastic and you will always remember this place with the beautiful view to the sea.
- I Cavaddari piazza Bellavista, +39 095 606 755 Not easy to find in the suburb of Santa Cateria - but look for the church and then the restaurant is next door. Dinner at this place is

really good: everything is absolutely fresh, taste combinations are stunning, appearance deserves five stars and the service is impeccable! Menu prices range between 32 and 40 euros per person and for the amount of fresh fish and sea food, it's well worth it!

- Bistrot la Framboisette Via Vittorio Emanuele II, 189, +39 348 245 5795 The staff is very friendly and always very keen on satisfying your every need. The staff is also very fluent in English, a rare quality here in Sicily. The food is fantastic, the ingredients are very fresh and also local. The recipes are traditional but also surprising. In short don't miss it!
- Casa del grecale Via S. Caterina, 53, +39 095 605 105 A place that leaves nothing to chance, from the food we try to revisit the classics in a modern Sicilian dishes, finishes the location they recreate successfully something unique. To commend the room staff but especially the director, a young ambitious who cures all so manically and tastefully trying to satisfy every desire of the customers.
- Re Dolce Freddo Via Giovanni Verga 53, +39 095 764 9298 One of the historical bars of the town Acese. Re Dolce Freddo is synonymous with quality products, courtesy, and be able to adapt to all customer needs. You can sample some of the best granite, the best almond paste, and is unbeatable in empty croissant, unique.
- L'oste scuro Piazza Lionardo Vigo, 5/6, +39 095 763 4001 This is a place to go eat. Excellent seafood, particularly the antipasto which two can share. Faces a lovely church. Service is fine and much cheaper than a restaurant in a major city. Mainly a seafood restaurant with good antipasti.
- Pizzeria Vecchia Stazione Viale Liberta' 24, +39 095 763 2115 The pizza is fantastic, with a large variety of pizza regarding the price they are very good value for money. They also make delivery service to hotels near by.
- La Stiva Via Nissoria 71 | Capomulini, +39 095 877214 Really simple restaurant with great fish and pizza. You can pick your own fresh fish and ask how you want it cooked. Very nice waiter! This is close to the sea and there are lots of restaurants in this street.

Catania

Fonte in Piazza Duomo

CATANIA, at the foot of Mt. Etna. Founded by the Greeks in 729 B.C., Catania became a Roman colony in 263 and was an important center during the reign of the Normans, Swabians and Bourbons. We shall start our tour through the town from the Piazza del Duomo with the fanciful Elephant Fountain in the middle.

Facing on to the square are the suggestive Palazzo del Municipio and the Baroque facade of the Cathedral by Vaccarini, the architect who reconstructed the most important buildings of Catania after the earthquake in 1693. The three original Apses of this once powerful medieval edifice (1169) can still be seen. Inside, rich works of art, medieval and Renaissance sculptures, and the Tomb of Vincenzo Bellini. Following Via Colombo and Via del Plebiscite, we come to the impressive Castello Ursino, a masterpiece of Swabian military architecture, which houses the

Museo Civico, with a rich collection of Greek and Roman sculptures, and the Picture Gallery.

Taking Via del Castello Ursino past Corso Garibaldi and Via Vittorio Emanuele, we turn to the right and enter the charming Via dei Crociferi, lined with delightful 18th century facades and balconies, Nearby, to the left, is the Greek Theatre and next to it the small Odeon. We then go along Via Einea, a stupendous straight street which has Mt. Etna as background. In Piazza Stesicoro we see the ruins of the Roman Amphitheatre and, further on, the lovely Bellini Gardens. Still keeping to the left, we walk to the huge 18th century church and convent of S. Nicolo all'Arena a monumental Baroque complex, dominated by the lofty dome of the church. We then descend to the Baroque Porta Garibaldi.

Where to eat in Catania:

Restaurants in Catania:
- Al Tortellino Via Giuseppe Simili 20/22, +39 095 532 186 Out of the city Centre, a place where the locals come to eat. The pasta is great and only €4. The pizzas huge and €5. Can't ask for better.
- Trattoria Catania Ruffiana Via Aloi, 50, +39 095 216 2222 This is a destination restaurant. Centrally located but not on the main walking street. The reviews on this place are spot on. Great food and extremely nice staff and you know you are getting truly homemade fresh Sicilian cuisine at a really good value. They even notate on their menu to specifically ask about certain fish being "fresh" as it can be seasonal.
- Don Mimi Via Umberto, 47, +39 095 250 0038 Very nice place especially during the summer. The food is really good and the cocktail are awesome! This place has very nice food. The portions are a bit small, I highly recommend ordering some of the starters or two course meal if you are really hungry. Not very cheap, but reasonable priced.
- Eat Pizzeria Via Coppola, 49/51, +39 095 310 100 Sure good pizza, and nothing more, but after all quality food. Only the location is a bit off but this should not keep you from visiting.

- Il Gusto della Mozzarella Via G. D'annunzio 164/A, +39 095 817 5644 Really good, all very good friendliness of staff, clean place, delicious mozzarella to go there every day
- Pausa Pranzo Corso delle Provincie 145, +39 095 716 8038 Excellent pizza and economical price. Quality ingredients. The restaurant is a bit small but clean and comfortable in a modern style with a few tables outside if you want to eat outside.
- Gisira Pizza and Drinks Via Gisira 62, +39 095 349 652 You were made to feel welcome the second you walked through the door. Amazing choice of pizzas. Great value and service. Cheese cake and tiramisu to die for. If you fancy something spicy try the Vulcano pizza. There usually is a queue of locals waiting to get a table. Take a good appetite with you. They also offer 1 meters pizzas to share from €20. Fantastic, best pizza ever
- Tenuta del Gelso Contrada Jungetto, +39 388 475 7488 You may have trouble finding the place, but this is to blame on your navigation system. Once we arrive you are taken care of by Ariana, who has good knowledge of the wines and the farm/ products in general. After a brief intro of the estate and a walk outside through the orange orchard you have a big lunch with all the local products they produce. You also have to taste 4 different wines and a dessert wine. This will be a great experience, totally worth it.
- Maurizio Pulvirenti Via Asiago, 40/40a/40b, +39 095 370 995 The place is very nice, clean and colorful! It is a typical Italian salumeria with a twist. During lunch and dinner time it transform itself into a really nice and welcoming restaurant, thanks especially to the owner and host! Very good people! Honest and hard worker! Prices are honest and not expensive at all, considering the quality of the food! Excellent!
- Il Vecchio Bastione Via Del Vecchio Bastione, 27, +39 095 310 903 A picturesque restaurant, charming environment down to the little details. Fantastic service and welcoming staff. Interesting menu and good choice of meals. This reasonably priced restaurant is a must for anyone in the area and is highly recommended.

Syracuse

Latomia del Paradiso

Syracuse. Founded in the 8th century B.C. on the tiny island of Ortygia, Syracuse was for centuries the largest and most powerful Greek city in the West which, under the rule of the tyrants Gelon, Hieron, Dionysius, Agothocles and Hieron II, had spread to the mainland. It declined with the Roman conquest and during the Middle Ages the inhabited area became confined once more to the island, though it regained some of its importance during the reigns of the Swabian and Aragonese kings. Devastated by the earthquake in 1693, it was partly rebuilt in its recent Baroque style.

We shall begin our tour with a visit to the archaeological monuments of the ancient town on the hill of Neapolis (the Greek word for "new city") where we find the Roman Amphitheater, a grandiose construction hollowed in the living rock at the time of Emperor Augustus.

Continuing upwards, beyond the small Norman church of S. Nicole, we see the altar of Hieron II to the left and, to the right, the ancient quarry with rocky walls known as the Latomia del Paradise, in which is the artificial cave called the Ear of Dionysius. Next to it, in a stupendous position overlooking the plain and the sea, is the Greek Theatre (467 B.C.), where Aeschylus, Pindar and Plato appeared.

Behind the Theatre rises a high rocky wall known as the Grotto of the Nymph, so called from a spring which still gushes from a cavern in the rock. We climb up the Via dei Sepolcri (the Street of Tombs) into the rocky sides of which are hewn the niches and tombs of an ancient necropolis. It is worth while continuing for another 5 miles on to the Castle of Euryalus, the mightiest and most complete fortress of Greek times, standing on the top of the Epipoli, the hill overlooking Syracuse.

On our way down, through Corso Galore, we come to Piazzale Marconi, where we find the ruins of the Roman Forum: following Corso Umberto I we cross the Ponte Nuevo over to the island of Ortygia where, in Piazza Pancali, we see the remains of a Temple of Apollo, the oldest of its kind in Sicily, which was later transformed into a mosque by the Arabs.

Through Via Savoia where, on the left, we pass the small 16th century Catalan church of S. Maria dei Miracoli with a remarkable portal, we come to Porta Marina, an arch in Spanish-Gothic style (15th century) which stands at the end of the Porto Grande (Great Harbor). Through the Foro Italico, we reach the famous Fountain of Arethusa, a freshwater spring on the seashore, celebrated in song by Pindar, Vergil, and many modern poets.

Continuing along the waterfront to the far end of the island, we reach the Maniace Castle, a beautiful Byzantine fortress which was enlarged under Frederick II. Returning to the fountain and through Via Capodieci, we come to the 13th century Palazzo Bellomo, which houses the Medieval Museum and a good Picture Gallery, where we must see the delightful Annunciation by Antonello da Messina.

We go on to Piazza del Duomo, which is lined with the ravishing facade of Barone edifices: the 17th century Palazzo del Municipio (Town Hall), the 18th century Palazzo Beneventano del Bosco whose Courtyard is a masterpiece of Syracuse Baroque architecture and the Museo Archeologico Nazionale, which contains one of the most important archaeological collections in Italy, with the magnificent Venus Anadyomene (also known as the Landolino Venus), sarcophagi, pottery, bronzes, etc.

The Cathedral has also a Baroque facade, but its severe and evocative interior is dominated by the impressive Doric column of the original Temple of Minerva. Among the numerous works of art, a panel by Antenello da Messina is of particular interest.

From the Piazza del Duomo, we reach the nearby Piazza Archimede, the heart of the city, with the Fountain) Artemis, the Palazzo Lanza with two-light Gothic windows, the building of the Banca d'Italia, and, on the corner of Via Montalto, the extremely beautiful Palazzo Montalto.

Syracuse: archeology

Syracuse, Greek Theatre

This will be a journey through time and space, following the traces of man's presence and activities in the basic periods of the ancient history of the Mediterranean. And the man who opened the scientific door to the discovery of the antiquity of this area of Sicily came from Trentino. Paolo Orsi arrived in Syracuse in 1886 and began the series of excavations in zones such as Stentinello, Thapsos, Castelluccio, Finocchito and Pantalica.

The pioneer of underwater archaeology along the Syracuse coast was Nino Lambogia from Liguria, who discovered the marble harbor of Syracuse. The "Orsi" Archaeological Museum of Syracuse contains 18,000 exhibits, arranged in strict chronological order, and including many pieces resulting from the research of these two archaeologists, and it is from these rooms that the itinerary must begin.

One of the masterpieces on show is the Venere Anadiomene, a second-century Roman copy of a statue of the Praxitelean school, praised by Guy de Maupassant. Not to be overlooked is the Sarcophagus of Adelphia, exhibited for the Giubileum; its base-reliefs, dating back to the VI century AD may be considered as the first nativity-scene of history. After the archaeological park of the Neapolis, with its Greek theatre, and the Greek necropolis of the Fusco, the archaeological journey continues towards the south.

Villa del Tellaro

Eight kilometers from Noto there are the defensive walls and the rectangular theatre. A kilometer away there is the Greek funeral monument, the Pizzuta column, and not far from there, the mosaics of the Roman Villa del Tellaro. The journey into the Iblean culture of the Siculi begins ten kilometers from Noto, with the traces of Finocchito, destroyed by the Syracusans in the V century. Further inland, there is the village of Castelluccio, from which the early Bronze age takes its name, where pottery with dark decorations on a yellowish background have been found.

At Palazzolo there is the archaeological park of Akrai, with its theatre, market-place and two stone-quarries. There is also the interesting series of the twelve Santoni, figures hewn out of the rock and dedicated to the Goddess Cybele. Near Akrai, there is the ancient Casmene. A few kilometers from Ferla, there is Pantalica, a natural fortress surrounded by an enormous necropolis in the midst of beautiful, wild countryside.

Further north, there is the city of Leontinoi, with its pincer system of fortification. Megara Hyblaea, destroyed by the Syracuse-ans and rebuilt by the Greeks to be destroyed once again by the Romans, looks out over the sea, while to the south there is perhaps what might be considered the most important discovery made by Orsi, the ancient village of Thapsos, dating back to between 1400 and 800 BC.

Where to eat in Syracuse:

Restaurants in Syracuse:

- Caseificio Borderi Via Emanuele de Benedictis, 6 | Mercato di Ortigia, +39 329 985 2500 Fantastic! This little gem of a lunch spot/deli is located in the fish markets of Syracuse, it is so good, word gets round quickly. The passion, pride and speed of the owners is astonishing. Yes you can queue for a while in the peak lunch hour however it's so worth it, plus the owner - a lovely happy gentleman comes around with bits of fresh buffalo mozzarella, smoked ricotta to nibble on. Always with a smile and twinkle in his eye. These are not just any panini's but filled with freshly cut prosciutto or salami, a variety of cheeses, semi-dried and fresh tomato, salads, you name it, the end result is high and delicious.
- Apollonion Osteria da Carlo Via Carmelo Campisi, 18, +39 0931 483 362 This is a delightful little restaurant serving a set tasting menu only. Everything is fresh and beautifully cooked. There is no choice, you simply get what you are given which at 35 Euros per person is amazing value. Water, dessert and coffee are included and for an extra 5 euros you can have house wine too.Be warned though, some of the seafood is uncooked/marinated in lemon juice, so you need to be prepared to try anything.
- Sicilia in Tavola via Cavour 28 | via Landolina, +39 246 10 889 First of all, you have to book. Just pass by or call and ask when you can get a table. The kind and helpful service will always find a solution; they speak at least Italian, English and French. The pasta are home made and the atmosphere is great. Fresh fish is served, following local fishing rules (hence the available fish dishes depends on the season).
- Le Vin de L'assassin Bistrot Roma 115, +39 093 166 159 The atmosphere is romantic and the owner, a french madame is really gently. One advise only is above the level of prices in Syracuse, for two person a standard dinner you go over 50 euros without wine. But need to be.
- Osteria Del Vecchio Ponte Via Luigi Greco Cassia, 7, +39 338 133 8894 Small family run restaurant. The "waiters" are father and daughter. Wife is responsible for checks. Very

good food, all of them very attentive. Wines are kind of modest. But, after all, I do not hesitate do recommend it strongly.

- Basirico Via Amalfitania, 56, 60, 62 | Cortile dei Bottai, +39 393 204 2023 A bright and cheerful restaurant there is a choice of more formal indoor dining and a more relaxed outdoor terrace, al-fresco experience. The food here is local, with big bold flavours which are great value. Staff are helpful and make dining here a real pleasure.
- Regina Lucia Piazza Duomo, 6 | Ortigia, +39 093 122 509 Located at the quieter end of the Piazza Duomo, the restaurant is a wonderful spot for dinner. Eating outside means having a great view of the Piazza too. Th seafood is very good, with all recommendations warmly received.
- Pizzeria-Trattoria Del Forestiero Corso Timoleonte n.2, +39 335 843 0736 Great Pizzas for a good price. Busy place with locals and policemen both eating in and carrying out. TV on all the time which is pretty authentic and a sign its a quality place!
- Retroscena Via Delle Maestranze 108, +39 0931 185 4278 A little off the main restaurant area but worth the detour. Interesting food in informal surroundings and with friendly owners. The restaurant is beautifully decorated with a gorgeous courtyard in the back.
- Trattoria del Buongustaio via Trieste 11, +39 0931 60197 All our dishes are delicious, but especially the seafood, which comes from the nearby markets. The English version of the menu provides some intriguing translations, e.g. "gouged mushrooms and sausage", "appetizer of warm sea" - but be assured that whatever is delivered to the table will be terrific. The friendly, efficient service and reasonable prices adds to your enjoyment.

Caltagirone

Caltagirone

On the morning of the next day, we leave Syracuse by Viale Ermocrate and, skirting the hill of Neapolis, we cross the Anapo river and drive uphill to Floridia (7 miles), and further up, through a harsh mountainous landscape to Palazzolo Acreide. Built on the site of the Syracuse colony of Acrae, this little town was destroyed by the earthquake in 1693 and rebuilt in its present Baroque style.

A charming Greek Theatre and an Odeon of the ancient town are well preserved. We now cross the Iblei Hills, pass through Buccheri and Vizzimi and, after 15 miles, we reach Grammichele. In spite of its modest appearance we must not forget that it presents one of the most important examples of Renaissance town planning; the hexagonal lay-out becomes clearly evident when seen from above and it might be a good idea, therefore, to try to find a photograph of the town plan.

After about 66 miles from Syracuse we come to CALTAGIRONE, beautifully situated on three hills. This little town, founded by the early Greeks, was reconstructed in the Baroque style after the earthquake of 1693. Worth seeing are: Via Cordova with its handsome Baroque facade, the neogothic church of S. Pietro and the church of S. Giacomo. From Caltarigone we take the road to PIAZZA ARMERINA (20 miles).

Piazza Armerina

Roman Bikinis at Piazza Armerina

Piazza Armerina (20 miles) and three miles after we reach the town, we have, to our left, the ruins of the Villa Romana del Casale, one of the most impressive archaeological sites in Sicily. The luxurious residence of millionaires during the times of the Roman Empire, it is famous, above all, for its marvelous mosaics, and especially for the one depicting ten girls wearing a garment which we thought was a modern invention, the bikini.

In the town of Piazza Armerina, founded by the Lombards during the Middle Ages, there is a stately 16th century Cathedral the lovely church of San Pietro, and the small 13th century church of S. Giovanni di Rodi.

Piazza Armerina

This villa is located near Piazza Armerina in south central Sicily. The beautiful floors are done entirely in mosaic.

The "Villa Romana del Casale" has already been, in 1997, declared from Unesco inalienable heritage of Mankind because it quite represents not just an extraordinary and important witness of the Roman lifestyle towards the end of the Empire but even the complex system of economic, social and cultural relations in which it was integrated with particular reference to the Mediterranean basin.

Through its mosaics it is possible to go again along the history of the greatest among the Empires, a sort of photographic album that shows not just the scenes of everyday life, but even representations of Divinities and Heroes, hunting scenes, cupids and children having races and others countless representations that leave the visitor amazed by the beauty of everything he can see.

Piazza Armerina

The villa, rising on an area of more then 3500 square meters, was probably the hunting residence of the Emperor Massimiliano, named Herculeos Victor; or the residence of an important roman patrician, maybe Valerio Proculo Populonio. It presents 48 rooms. Almost in every room it is possible to see the splendid mosaics made almost certainly by north African workers that used to utilize this technique. The structure was made between the end of the III Century and the beginning of the IV. The first diggings of scientific importance were undertaken by the Municipality of Piazza Armerina in 1881 and abandoned soon after.

Later they were resumed between 1935 and 1939 but just in 1954 the Villa begun to be dug out by the means of the great archaeologist Gino Vinicio Gentili. Thanks to the digging, lasting no less than 9 years, he gave to the world one of the most amazing and inestimable jewel of the history of art. Inhabited even during the Arabic age, the Villa was partially destroyed by the Normans. Afterwards, an avalanche of mud, coming from the Mount Mangone (raising above the Villa) covered it almost totally. The morphology of the ground conditioned and determined the plan metric development of the structure, giving to it an organization on three levels.

The Villa follow the slope of the hill on which it rises, determining architectonic peculiarities really remarkable. It is divided into several parts: the residential zone (built around the big central peristyle over which overlook even the basilica, reserved to the official receptions); an official zone with the elliptical peristyle (xistus) and the big trilobite lounge (triclinio); the whole of the thermae with the aqueduct that provided to its watering.

The polygonal courtyard that is the entrance to the Villa act as a Hinge between the zones in which it is subdivided. All the pictures, executed with the mosaic technique, deserve to be admired. Among them the more popular are: in the "Ambulacro della Grande Caccia" (the hall of the Great Hunting), the capture and the transport of the animals destined to the circus games; in the vestibule, the fight among Eros and Pan and the portrayal of Ulisse and Polifemo; in the triclinium the labors of Hercules. Surely the best known picture is that one of the girls wearing Bikinis.

It is situated in one of the rooms to the South of the peristyle. The Villa is easy to reach through the motorway Palermo-Catania, leaving the motorway at the Enna or Mulinello Junction and continuing towards the city of Piazza Armerina; it is even possible to use the railway links Palermo-Catania.

We continue our drive through a beautiful landscape of solitary hills, past the junction for Enna on our right (17 miles from Piazza Armerina) and, after 13 more miles, we come to CALTANISSETTA (l18 miles from Syracuse). In Piazza Garibaldi stands the Baroque Cathedral with a lavishly decorated interior. It would be advisable to eat lunch in Caltanissetta before taking the road which, through Serradifalco and Canicatti, descends amidst vineyards almond and olive groves, to AGRIGENTO.

Where to eat in Piazza Armerina:

Restaurants in Piazza Armerina

- Azienda Agrituristica Savoca Restaurant Contrada Leano, +39 328 004 2912 Everything is perfect: the food and service. The elegance and nature reign supreme. They manage to make, with their perfect simplicity, unforgettable one of the most important days of your life. They make you feel at home. Recommended to anyone looking for somewhere peaceful and family who want to relax, enjoy and spend a pleasant day in good company.

- Cafe des Amis via marconi, 22, +39 0935 682 072 This not a restaurant but a small cafe with about four tables. The arancini are delicious as are the cannoli and biscotti. The owner and his family make you feel welcome and give you a lot of freebies!

- Al Fogher Strada Statale 117/BIS, +39 0935 684123 This is a first rate restaurant with a chef passionate about fusing flavours with local ingredients. The Maitre'D had worked in London and is very helpful in explaining the mid-sized menu and the 400 strong wine list. All the food is cooked and presented with care and skill.

- Trattoria Da Gianna Commenda dei Cavalieri di Malta, +39 347 3064581 Situated next to the Garibaldi Theatre, all tables are outdoors but undercover. The menu is not extensive, but the pasta is fantastic. Staff speak no English, but that is not a problem.

- Guendalina Ristorante Piazzale Luigi Capuana, +39 0935 686583 Local tastefully decorated cozy at times refined, and for all budgets. Great service, good pizza.

- Trattoria Al Goloso Via Garao, 4 | Piazza Garibaldi, +39 0935 684325 When passion meets simplicity in Italian cuisine the result is sublime. Few ingredients, limited but well thought choice ensures the great quality of this place. In an open kitchen in the middle of the restaurant the chef prepares the dishes for you...from a to z. Prices very (too) convenient.

Agrigento

Agrigento

Agrigento. Founded in 582 B.C., Agrigento flourished under the reign of the tyrant Therone (488-473) but was destroyed by the Carthaginians and finally occupied and rebuilt by the Romans in 210 B.C.

It was a majestic and large city which comprised all of the hill (the center of the present town), where probably the Acropolis stood, and the so called Valley of the Temples, which was enclosed by 7 1/2 miles of walls.

During the Middle Ages, only the hill town existed and it first started spreading downhill in modern times. In the upper town, we will visit the imposing Monastery of S. Spirito (1290), built in Gothic style with elegant decorations and the extremely rich and very important. National Archaeological Museum close at hand.

In the modern town, we pass by the beautiful Gothic church of S. Nicola, in the ancient Greek-Roman quarter, beyond which begins the Valley of the Temples. There were once about 20 temples, the ruins of which are in various states of preservation.

We notice immediately the Temple of Hercules, with archaic capitals. On the right side of the road, we now see the colossal Olympieion (Temple of Olympian Jove) and, beyond it, the picturesque corner of the Temple o Castor and Pollux.

Beyond the Temple of Hercules, in a beautiful olive grove, is the so-called Tomb of Theron, Turning left, we come to the gem of, ancient Agrigento, the so-called Temple of Concord, which rivals in beauty and perfect preservation the temples of Paestum and even the Theseion at Athens. The magnificent structure is rendered even more majestic by the high steps of the plinth upon which it rests and by the gentle landscape in which it stands. The last of the large temples, the Temple of Juno Lacinia, is standing on a hill surrounded by olive trees.

Agrigento Temple

Two of the great cities of Magna Graecia — or what's left of them — can be explored along Sicily's southern coast. Both Agrigento and Selinunte knew greater glory than they experience today, but the remains of what they used to be are still relatively rich in spite of the looters and conquerors who have passed through. Of the two, Agrigento is the far greater attraction.

Once known as the Greek city of Akragas, **Agrigento** has seen many conquerors in its day, from the Romans to Byzantines and Arabs. The year 1087 saw the arrival of the Normans.

Agrigento's remarkable series of Doric temples from the 5th century B.C. are unrivaled except in Greece itself. All of the modern encroachments, especially the hastily built and often illegal new buildings, have seriously dimmed the glory of Agrigento, but much is left to fill us with wonder.

Ancient Akragas covers a huge area – much of which is still un-excavated today – but is exemplified by the famous "Valley of the Temples" (actually a misnomer, as it is a ridge, rather than a valley).

This comprises a large sacred area on the south side of the ancient city where seven monumental Greek temples in the Doric style were constructed during the 6th and 5th centuries BC. Now excavated and partially restored, they constitute some of the largest and best preserved ancient Greek buildings outside of Greece itself. They are listed as a World Heritage Site.

The best preserved of the temples are two very similar buildings traditionally attributed to the goddesses Juno Lacinia and Concordia (though archaeologists believe this attribution to be incorrect). The latter temple is remarkably intact, due to its having been converted into a Christian church in 597 CE. Both were constructed to a peripteral hexastyle design. The area around the Temple of Concordia was later re-used by early Christians as a catacomb, with tombs hewn out of the rocky cliffs and outcrops.

"It was scarcely possible to be more judicious and fortunate than the Agrigentines were in the choice of a situation for a large city; they were here provided with every requisite for defense, pleasure, and comfort of life; a natural wall, formed by abrupt rocks, presented a strong barrier against assailants; pleasant hills sheltered them on three sides without impeding the circulation of air; before them a broad plain watered by the Acragas, an agreeable stream from which the city took its name, gave admittance to the sea-breeze...... the port or emporium lay in view at the mouth of the river...."

Henry Swinburne, *Travels in the Two Sicilies*

Where to eat in Agrigento:

Restaurants in Agrigento

- La Posata Di Federico II Piazza Cavour, 19 | Viale della Vittoria, +39 0922 28289 / +39 348 5481497 Magnificent! Fresh produces ,everything cooked with love and attention ,wonderful atmosphere , excellent service. This is a restaurant not to be missed. It's a mom and pop operation, but on the highest level. The cuisine is very refined.

- Kalos Salita filino 1, +39 0922 26389 Typical Sicilian food prepared with an elegant touch, imaginative menu, lovely room and balcony dining. Pretty much upscale but very reasonably priced.

- Agriturismo Oasi Valle Lupo Contrada Valle Lupo, 8 | Strada Provinciale 64, +39 338 656 9784 Off the main highway and onto a small farm road there is a large remote house on the side of a hill. Everything is well prepared and delicious, the wine is superb and the service impeccable. Everything was done to perfection. If you are in the area don't pass this up.

- Il Re di Girgenti Via Panoramica dei Templi, 51 +39 0922 401388 The food is excellent, all 3 courses, the staff great, the ambience superb, and the view of the valley of the temples of the greek gods is amazing at night. They have a terrace or you can eat in very nice interior.

- Naif Via Vela 8, +39 0922 187 0735 If you are lucky enough to get an outdoor table, it is in a beautiful courtyard just up a few steps from Via Atenea. The husband and wife team who are front of house are a delight with charming advice and professional service.

Porto Empedocle

Porto Empedocle – La Scala dei Turchi

The next morning we drive west out of Agrigento for about 5 miles to Porto Empedocle, from where the road follows the coast of southern Sicily with its numerous beaches and bathing resorts.

We come, through Montallegro (where nearby the ruins of the ancient city of Heracleia Minoa have been recently excavated); then through Ribera and 43 miles from Agrigento, through Sciacca, with the church of S. Margherim (portal by Laurana) and the 15th century Palazzo Steripinto with rusticated walls, and Menfi.

About 66 miles from Agrigento, we reach a junction where we take the road towards the sea which, after 3 miles, leads us to ruins of SELINUNTE.

Selinunte

Selinunte

Selinunte, in contrast, was never built over as Agrigento was, and holds extensive remains of the acropolis, though none quite equal the charm of Agrigento's Valley of the Temples.

As you stand in the midst of a carpet of mandrake, acanthus, capers, and celery growing wild at Selinunte, you'll have to work hard to imagine what the city must have looked like at the apex of its power.

According to the Athenian historian Thucydides, Selinus was founded by people from Megara Hyblaea, a city on the east coast of Sicily, in the 7th century BC. The city had a very short life (about 200 years). During this time its population grew to a total of about

25,000. A wealthy trade center, Selinus was envied by the Carthaginians.

Selinunte

Selinus had an almost permanent conflict with Segesta, which allied itself with Athens. However, the Athenians were defeated by the Syracuse-ans, and Segesta now asked help from Carthage.

Diodorus Siculus tells that the Carthaginian commander Hannibal (not to be confused with his more famous namesake), in 409 BC destroyed Selinus after a war that counted about 16,000 deaths and 5,000 prisoners. The city was besieged for nine days by an army of 100,000 Carthaginians.

SELINUNTE. This was once a town which represented the furthermost point of Greek penetration into the territory of Carthage and was destroyed by the Carthaginians in 250 B.C.

The grandiose solitary ruins, on the shores of the sea, constitute one of the most impressive attractions of Magna Graecia. We take the same road back to the junction and continue on inland to CASTELVETRANO. In this town which is of medieval origin, there is a delightful Renaissance church, the Chieso Madre, and an outstanding Baroque interior in the church of San Domenico. About 2 miles west of the town, there is the famous Norman church of the Trimta (or of Delia). From Castelvetrano, the road goes through S. Nina and Salemi (16 miles) and passes the outskirts of Calatafimi, from where it leads us to the ruins of SEGESTA.

SEGESTA, another evocative Greek town. It was destroyed by the Byzantines and only a Temple and a Theatre have remained, standing on Monte Barbaro in majestic and silent solitude. About 34 miles from Castelvetrano, we reach ALCAMO, a picturesque medieval town, overlooking the Tyrrhenian Sea and the Gulf of Castellammare. In the upper part of Alcamo, there is a Castle and further down we find the 16th century church of the Madonna dei Miracoli, the church of San Tommaso with its Gothic facade, and numerous medieval and Baroque buildings. From Alcamo the road descends to Partinico (12 miles) and after another 18 miles we reach Monreale, which we will visit on the last day. Through the enchanting scenery of the Conca d'Oro, amidst magnificent orange groves, we are now coming to the capital of Sicily PALERMO.

Palermo

Palermo

PALERMO. An ancient Phoenician base, Palermo became a Roman city in 253 A.D. After the Barbarian invasion, it was dominated, in turn, by the Byzantines, the Arabs, an We will begin our tour of the town at the richly ornamented Porta Nuova, at the end of Corso Vittorio Emanuele. To the right, in the middle of a vast garden, stands the Palazzo Reale, built by the Norman King Roger II, from whose-time nothing remains on the outside, but the Tower of S. Ninfa; the vast facade was rebuilt during the Baroque period.

We enter a handsome 17th century Courtyard, from which a great staircase leads to the Cappella Palatina, the jewel of ArabNorman art (1140) with delightful mosaics on a gold ground which shines in the rich and and mysterious half-light and with a wooden ceiling in the central nave, which is a splendid example of Arab workmanship. On the next floor are the royal apartments with Baroque and neoclassical decorations.

Leaving the palace, we come to the nearby church of S. Giovanni degli Eremiti, which was likewise built by Roger II. Its round red domes and the luxuriant, tropical vegetation of the enchanting cloister evoke the delicate image of some distant corner of the Orient. We proceed to Piazza della Vittoria, where we see the superb Palazzo Sclafani, whose noble 14th century facade faces Piazza S. Giovanni. We return to Corso Vittorio Emanuele and arrive in Piazza della Cattedrale.

Palermo Cathedral

The Cathedral, which dominate this square, has been built and rebuilt in several styles over the centuries. The original building dates from 1185, but the dome, beautiful in itself, though out of keeping with the rest of the edifice, was built by the architect Ferdinando Fuga at the end of the 18th century. On the right side, there is an impressive Gothic arcade and an elaborate Portal by Gambara (15th century). The facade dates essentially from the 14th and 15th centuries and is connected by two pointed arches with the curious bell-tower opposite, which was restored in the 19th century.

The interior, unfortunately restored by the architect of the dome, Ferdinando Fuga, contains the majestic, but solemn, Tombs of the Norman and Swabian Kings, of which the most important is that of Frederick II of Swabia, the greatest monarch in Europe after Julius Caesar. We now continue down Corso Vittorio Emanuele, towards the center of town.

To the right, we have the church of S. Salvatore with a lavish interior, and further on the church of S. Giuseppe dei Teatini, richly adorned with marbles, frescoes and stuccoes. We have thus reached the Quattro Canti (Four Corners), the scenographic crossroads of Corso Vittorio Emanuele and the magnificent Via Maqueda the heart of Baroque Palermo.

Palermo

Across Via Maqueda, on the right side, we come to Piazza Pretoria where, apart from the monumental Tuscan Renaissance

Fountain, we sec the facade of the Palazzo del Municipio (Town Hall). In the adjacent Piazza Bellini, we find the churches of S. Caterina, an elegant, purely Baroque edifice, and S. Maria dell'Ammiraglio (known as La Martorana) which behind its Baroque facade preserves a splendid Norman interior (1143) with Mosaics, interrupted here and there by interior 18th century frescoes.

We must sec the charming Cloister and note the elegant 12th century Bell-tower, the most beautiful Arab-Norman structure in Palermo, before visiting the nearby church of San Cataldo (1160), another masterpiece of Arab-Norman architecture, with an austere interior and three red domes in Saracen style. We then go back to Via Maqueda and, following a small lane, across this street, we come to Piazza Quaranta Martiri where stands Palazzo Marchesi with a magnificent Gothic Courtyard and a 15th century Tower which rises next to the Baroque bell-tower of the adjacent Casa Professa (or Gesu).

We now return to Piazza Bellini, from where we take the Discesa dei Giudici and, past the church of Sant'Anna. continue straight to Piazza Rivoluzione and the nearby Palazzo Aiutamicristo, which has a magnificent Portico in the courtyard. Behind the Palace is the church of SS. Trinita (also called the Magione), from which we will go in the direction of the harbour, through the ancient Arab quarter of the Kalsa. In Via Torremura we pass the church of S. Teresa and, at the corner of Via Alloro, the church of Madonna della Pieta, with the most beautiful Baroque facade in Palermo which resembles that of churches in Rome of the same period. Along the narrow old Via Altoro lined with beautiful palaces, we come to the Gothic-Renaissance Palazzo Abbatellis with a Tower.

The Palace houses the National Gallery of Sicily where we may admire the fresco, Triumph of Death, from the second half of the 15th century, paintings by Antonello da Messina and his school, by Gossaert, and by Garofalo, ceramics and sculpture by Giunta, Pisano, and particularly the magnificent bust of Eleonora of Aragon, by Lantana.

Not far from the Museum is the Church of S. Maria degli Angell (known as La Gancia) with a 15th century- Invade and a richly decorated interior. On the right side of the nearby Piazza Marina stands the 14th century Palazzo Chiaramonte and near the harbour, the church of S. Maria della Catena.

Returning to Piazza Marina with the Garibaldi Gardens in the center, we notice the Palazzo San Cataldo and the small church of S. Maria dei Miracoli, both built in Renaissance style. Along Via Merlo we come to the magnificent Gothic church of San Francesco d'Assisi (13th century) with a fine rose window in the facade and beautiful Renaissance choir-stalls and sculptures in the interior. Near by is the Oratorio di San Lorenzo, whose stucco decoration of the interior is the masterpiece of Giacomo Serpotta.

The Vucciria Market

Vucciria market

The Vucciria, in the heart of Palermo's historic old city, opens early. By 4 a.m., fishermen are hauling in the day's catch; by 5 a.m., vendors are setting out crates of fruit and vegetables; and by

6 a.m., the place is bustling with shoppers. It's a tradition that's gone on, more or less the same way, for the last 700 years.

Every day but Sunday, the Vucciria fills with fishermen, shopkeepers and merchants who have come to peddle their goods. And it's quite a selection: pasta, grains, sacks of beans, bags of dried herbs, shoes, socks, cigarette lighters shaped like handguns, grappa, wine, CDs, paintings and paperweights of the Madonna, salted capers (a local specialty), zucchini the size of a child's leg, crates of artichokes still attached to their long stalks, tomatoes (large, small, sun-dried, packed in oil, in a can, on the vine) and practically anything else you can think of.

Where to eat in Palermo:

Restaurants in Palermo

- Villa Ermes Via Corrado Martinez, 1 | Via San Lorenzo 300, +39 091 671 2557 The location is fantastic, an old villa surrounded by greenery, with a beautiful garden, in San Lorenzo, but absolutely out of traffic, car horns and annoying noises of the city! There is a virtually private parking.

- Al Fondaco del Conte Piazza Conte Federico, 24, +39 091 652 2312 5 This restaurant is not easy to find, but is well worth the looking. Two brothers and a sister run this family restaurant right in the centre of Palermo, and the cooking is imaginative and interesting. Tasty and imaginative food at al fondaco, all made in house, including the pasta.

- Sesto Canto Via Sant'oliva 26, +39 091 324543 True, this restaurant offers a wide array of traditional and revisited versions of Sicilian cuisine as well other day specials, based on what they bought in the market that day. The decoration is clean, the restaurant is well lit and the music - mostly jazz - makes for a very cozy and relaxing atmosphere.

- Carizzi d'Amuri Via Lungarini 21, +39 329 134 1439 The restaurant is stylish and the atmosphere is peaceful and calm. Not the place where you show up in shorts and sandals. The dinner at Carizzi d'Amuri is a perfection in all matters - the location, staff, wine, food and the very friendly good night.

- Trattoria ai Cascinari Via D'Ossuna 43-45, +39 091 651 9804 Not very central,10 minutes walk from the royal Palace, there is this traditional place with many rooms and lot of tasty fishes and pastas. Warm welcome.

- Trattoria I Compari Corso Domenico Scina 82, +39 389 056 6047 A true local place. When you wander in you will be greeted and treated warmly by the host and all staff. No question: most probably you will be the only non-Palermitans there. Good, reliable basic dishes and a fun atmosphere.

Solunto

Solunto

It should not yet be too late in the afternoon to take a trip to Monte Pellegrino or to the ruins of SOLUNTO, an ancient GraecoRoman city on the sea at Cape Zafferano near Bagheria. On our second day inPalermo, we will start from Piazza Quattro Canti and walk down from Maqueda to Piaz. On the way back, we go to Piazza Olivella, to visit the National Archaeological Museum.

Set in a former convent with lovely rooms and courtyards, it contains the most remarkable and important collection of Greek antiquities in Italy with countless sculptures, mosaics, ceramics. coins, and, above all, the celebrated Metopes from the temples of Selinunte.za Verdi and the Teatro Massimo, to have a look at the modern town.

Leaving the Museum, we go to the Piazza San Domenico with the beautiful Baroque church of San Domenico and from there to S. Maria la Nuova (16th century).

In the afternoon, we will first visit the Palace known as La Zisa, one of the few secular buildings remaining intact from the Norman period, which we reach from Porta Nuova by way of Via Colonna Rotta and Via Zisa, Then, taking Via dei Cipressi, we come to the famous Convento dei Cappuccini, once the burial place of the wealthy citizens of Palermo whose remains, reduced to skeletons, create a scene which is at once gruesome and grotesque. We return to Porta Nuova and follow Corso Calatafimi. At No. 94, inside the Tukory Barracks, we find the Cuba, another Norman palace (1180), which was built on the model of the Zisa and whose dome is visible even from the street.

The rest of the afternoon we will use for visiting the wonderful Cathedral of Monreale. We follow the straight Corso Calatafimi which, climbing slightly, takes us (5 miles from the center of Palermo) to Monreale.

Monreale

Duomo Cloister

MONREALE. Originally an Arab village, this small town grew up round the Cathedral built by William II in 1174. It is the most beautiful Norman church in Sicily and one of the most fabulous architectural works of the Middle Ages. The three-arch arcade in the facade, however, dates from the 18th century.

We should start our visit by walking round the outside of the church to admire the three apses, with their warm brownish hue, the finest architectural part of the building. We enter the church through the main portal with bronze doors by Bonanno Pisano (1186), or through the side portal with bronze doors of the same period, and no less beautiful, by Barisano da Trani.

The stately interior, which rest on 18 columns from Roman temples, is adorned with the most magnificent mosaics in Southern Italy, representing the whole cycle of the Old and New Testaments, and converging on the enormous figure of Christ (Pantocrator) in the apse.

To conclude, we must visit the enchanting Cloister.

Sicily Food & Recipes

Melagrana - pomegranate

On any given night, Sicilian families can be found passing around a heaping plate of **caponata**, a traditional antipasto made of eggplant, tomatoes, celery, olives, and capers. Fisherman used to devour this dish with seafood at the end of a long fishing day, but caponata has evolved into one of the most popular Sicilian dishes. The recipe varies and sometimes includes artichokes and even chocolate.

No contemporary Italian kitchen would be complete without a bottle of **Marsala wine**. But centuries ago, this cooking staple was created in the western Sicilian town of Marsala to challenge the Portuguese and Spanish monopoly on fortified wines such as Madeira and sherry. Today, *marsala* is used all over the world to enhance the flavor of a dish, create a sauce, or to be enjoyed as a dessert wine.

Produced in the province of Ragusa and several towns near Syracuse, **Caciocavallo Ragusano** (*Cosacavaddu Rausanu* in Sicilian dialect) is a traditional Sicilian cheese made by curdling cow's milk inside a wooden container called a "tina," cooking the curds, and then kneading or pulling them by hand. The name was inspired by the practice of tying cheese (*cacio* in Italian) two-by-two and hanging them so that they straddle (a *cavallo* in Italian) a wooden beam to age. The seasoned variety is used in many traditional Sicilian recipes, especially pasta and bean dishes.

It's impossible to resist the spell of a Sicilian pastry shop window with its explosion of tantalizing colors and aromas. Among the vast array of Sicilian pastry products, the place of honor definitely goes to the *cassata*. Made of a tantalizing mixture of sponge cake, chocolate, sweetened ricotta, candied fruit, and nuts, the *cassata* is usually decorated with thick icing or marzipan and covered with brightly colored candied fruits.

The ever-popular **cannoli**, fried pastry rolls with a delicious filling made from sweet ricotta, chocolate and candied fruits, were once a treat only at Carnival time, but now are enjoyed year-round. And no festival in Sicily would be complete without **torrone**, the mouthwatering honey-and-nuts nougat that is made in a wide range of varieties across the island.

Sicily Food: Sicilian speciality recipes

Agghiotta di pesce spada - Swordfish cooked with tomato, pine nuts, raisins, olives and herbs.

Arancini di riso - Fried rice balls with a core of cheese, peas, chopped meats and tomatoes

Bottarga – Tuna roe

Braccioli di pesce spada – Grilled swordfish fillets wrapped around a cheese-vegetable filling.

Bruschetta ai Capperi di Pantelleria – Pantelleria Capers Bruschetta

Cannoli con ricotta – Ricotta-stuffed Rolls

Caponata siciliana – Eggplant and Tomato Stew

Carciofi ripieni – Artichokes stuffed with sausage, sardines and cheese and baked.

Cassata alla siciliana – Sicilian Cassata

Cotognata – Quince Preserve

Couscous con pesce – Fish Stew Couscous

Crispeddi – Anchovy and Dill Fritters

Fravioli di Carnevale – Fried sweet ravioli filled with ricotta and cinnamon.

Falsomagro – Stuffed Beef Roll

Gnocculli – semolino gnocchi with ricotta and meat sauce.

Gnocculli di San Giuseppe – semolino gnocchi with eggs, cinnamon and sugar.

Involtini di pesce spada – Swordfish Rolls
Melanzane alla siciliana – Eggplant fried and then baked with mozzarella and tomato sauce.
Panizza – Chickpea Polenta
Pasta alla Norma – spaghetti with a sauce of eggplant and tomato
Pasta con le sarde – Bucatini with Sardines
Peperonata - bell peppers stewed with onion, tomato and olives, often served cold.
Pesce spada a'sammorigghu – Grilled Swordfish
Pesto ericino – Pesto from Erice
Pignolata or pignulata – Confection of sweet fried dumplings (sometimes chocolate coated).
Polpettone siciliano – meatball of ground beef, breadcrumbs, grated cheese and eggs, fried in olive oil and served with tomato sauce.
Salmoriglio – Olive Oil, Lemon and Garlic Sauce
Sarde a beccafico – Stuffed Sardines
Scorzette di arance candite – Candied orange peels.
Sfincioni or sfinciuni – Thick focacce with tomato and cheese, specialty of Palermo
Spaghetti alla Puttanesca – Spaghetti "*Whore style*"
Testina di capretto al forno – Baked Spring Kid's Head
Zite al pomodoro e tonno – Short pasta tubes with tomato and tuna sauce.

The Author

Enrico Massetti was born in Milano. Now he lives in Washington DC, USA, but he regularly visit his hometown, and enjoys going around all the places near his home town that can be reached by public transportation.

Enrico can be reached at enricomassetti@msn.com.

Other tourist e-guides

One day outings from Milan without a car

One day Outings from Milan without a car

Florence in two days

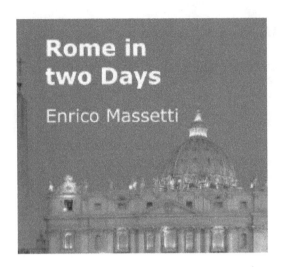

Rome in two days

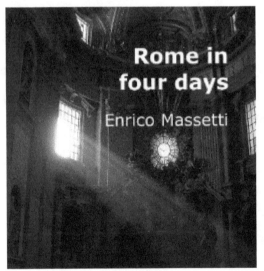

Rome in four days

Venice in two,
three or more days

Enrico Massetti

Venice in two days

Photo Credits

Duomo – Photo © Stefania
Duomo – Photo © Angelo Miceli
Duomo Bell Tower – Photo © Angelo Miceli
Fountain of Nettuno – Photo © Angelo Miceli
Galleria Vittorio Emanuele – Photo © HEN Magonza
The "Badiazza" – Photo © Giulia Gasparro
Lipari – Photo © Sossio
Vulcano – Photo © Edoardo dalla Nora
Vulcano – Photo © Luciana Coletti -*Elle*
Vulcano – Photo © Luciana Coletti -*Elle*
Lipari – Photo © Sossio
Taormina – Photo © Photo Alessandro Rossi
Taormina and Mount Etna – Photo © Miguelftorres
Acireale Santa Tecla – Photo © Francesco Pappalardo
Fonte in Piazza Duomo – Photo © Sigismondo Novello
Latomia del Paradiso – Photo © Dominic Torrisi
Syracuse, Greek Theatre – Photo © MarianOne
Villa del Tellaro – Photo © Rebecca Dru
Caltagirone – Photo © Carlo Manni
Roman Bikinis at Piazza Armerina – Photo © Mauro Manmano
Piazza Armerina – Photo © Mauro Manmano
Piazza Armerina – Photo © Mauro Manmano
Agrigento – Photo © Pachebel Canon
Agrigento Temple – Photo © laurenz
Porto Empedocle – La Scala dei Turchi – Photo © myriapod
Selinunte – Photo © pablolemosochandio
Selinunte – Photo © pablolemosochandio
Palermo – Photo © Carla
Palermo Cathedral – Photo © Angelo Miceli
Palermo – Photo © Giordano Mangione
Vucciria market – Photo © Beppe Modica
Solunto – Photo © psub
Duomo Cloister – Photo © Andrea Rapisarda

Table of Contents

CPSIA information can be obtained
at www.ICGtesting.com
Printed in the USA
BVHW051700060722
641477BV00004B/105